# 100 POEMS TO CELEBRATE GROWING OLDER

To Casper and Red Rum, who are both getting older,
and also to Matilda, with all my love

# 100 POEMS TO CELEBRATE GROWING OLDER

EDITED BY JANE MCMORLAND HUNTER

BATSFORD

# Introduction

This anthology opens with a poem which looks forward and ends with one which looks back. Both views are important as one grows older but so, too, is the present and, in between, this collection includes poems which encourage the reader to seize the day and make the most of the present.

Many people live longer now than in the past and perceptions of old age have changed – sometimes for the better, sometimes not. In some societies, the elders are highly regarded for their knowledge and memories; in others they are seen as a problem, a part of the population to be dealt with, rather than respected. The views of poets have also changed. Historically, many did not live to see old age: William Shakespeare died at fifty-five, Anne Brontë at a mere twenty-nine. Until Victorian times love and death dominated the themes of poetry, with old age being regarded as something to be endured, 'sans teeth', etc. I have included poems from the sixteenth century to the present day, but have tried to shift the emphasis towards a positive outlook.

Inevitably as one ages there is the temptation to look back – particularly to the 'good old days'. Several of these poets look back over entire lifetimes, including Thomas Love Peacock and Lucy Larcom, often through the proverbial rose-tinted spectacles. It is important to remember, but probably not to regret;

our lives contain too many choices to worry about things we have not done, we cannot tell what would have been on the roads we did not take.

The experience of old age is unique to each person – in one poem twenty-eight or nine is regarded as 'really old' while, in the world of elves, it takes three score years and ten before one is entitled to a coat with buttons and pockets. Some of the poems compare youth and old age, but some of the attitudes are surprising; Robert Herrick sees the benefits of growing older, as does Patricia Beer, and D. H. Lawrence gives a power to the old over the young, even if it is one of spite.

Life inevitably changes and many things we took for granted become more challenging or even impossible, but, along with memories, we also gain experience, calmness and wisdom. And then there is responsibility – as we age do we become more responsible or do we feel the rules regarding our behaviour become more relaxed? A well-known poem advocates wearing purple and others in this collection suggest eccentricity and paddling. One of the possible titles for this collection was 'growing old disgracefully'. It was discarded as not all the poems advocate bad behaviour, but it seems old age can bestow a certain freedom – no more striving to do well or worrying about what other people think.

The speed at which we notice it may vary, but no one can escape the passing of time. An inscription on a church in Kent recognises the fickleness of time – creeping in childhood, walking and running as we grow, and finally flying as we approach old age. Childhood, adolescence, grown-up, middle-aged and old are all labels, but they happen to each individual differently and at different times. It is not so much when it arrives as how we deal with each stage that matters. There seem to be two main approaches: make a to-do list and work through it or enjoy life as it is. Either can be right. I feel a good approach is to make the most of what one has – laughing, dancing and happiness. Some poets, such as Elaine Feinstein, even find there are positive advantages to old age; love is still possible, indeed for some it is just starting, and one optimistic suitor even suggests marriage.

The poems come from a variety of sources, including the music hall, the Bible and the plays of William Shakespeare. Many are famous, others less well known. What I hope they all do, through reflection, humour and hope, is to make the reader view growing older in a positive light.

Perhaps surprisingly, old age is also a good time to look forward, with poets recommending hope, optimism and laughter as useful attitudes. Of course, the unavoidable point in the future is death, but how one approaches it is what really matters, regardless of any beliefs. Alfred, Lord Tennyson, Elizabeth Porter Gould and Chief Tecumseh all recommend different approaches, and one group of friends in their forties plan to henna their hair and go out in a last wild blaze. A common theme seems to be to try to live one's life so one does not fear the end. This is not an anthology about death but it recognises that it is one of the certainties of life. We need to be able to cope with this and enjoy our lives right up to the last moment.

End is in beginning;
And in beginning end:
Death is not loss, nor life winning;
But each to each is friend.
The hands which give are taking;
And the hands which take bestow:
Always the bough is breaking
Heavy with fruit or snow.

**'Song' by William Soutar (1898–1943)**

'stand upon the threshold of the new'

**Old Age**
Edmund Waller

## Promise

Remember, the time of year
when the future appears
like a blank sheet of paper
a clean calendar, a new chance.
On thick white snow

you vow fresh footprints
then watch them go
with the wind's hearty gust.
Fill your glass. Here's tae us. Promises
made to be broken, made to last.

**Jackie Kay** (1961–)

# A Petition to Time

Touch us gently, Time!
  Let us glide adown thy stream
Gently, – as we sometimes glide
  Through a quiet dream!
Humble voyagers are We,
Husband, wife, and children three –
(One is lost, an angel, fled
To the azure overhead!)

Touch us gently, Time!
  We've not proud nor soaring wings:
Our ambition, our content,
  Lies in simple things.
Humble voyagers are We,
O'er Life's dim, unsounded sea,
Seeking only some calm clime; –
Touch us gently, gentle Time!

**Bryan Waller Procter** (1787-1874)

## Think not of the future

Think not of the future, the prospect is uncertain;
Laugh away the present, while laughing
hours remain:
Those who gaze too boldly through Time's
mystic curtain
Soon will wish to close it, and dream of joy again.
I, like thee, was happy, and, on hope relying,
Thought the present pleasure might revive again;
But receive my counsel! time is always flying,
Then laugh away the present, while laughing
hours remain

I have felt unkindness, keen as that which hurts thee;
I have met with friendship fickle as the wind;
Take what friendship offers ere its warmth deserts thee;
Well I know the kindest may not long be kind.

Would you waste the pleasure of the summer season,
Thinking that the winter must return again?
If our summer's fleeting, surely that's a reason
For laughing off the present, while laughing
hours remain.

Thomas Haynes Bayly (1797–1839)

## I stepped from Plank to Plank

I stepped from Plank to Plank
A slow and cautious way
The Stars about my Head I felt
About my Feet the Sea.

I knew not but the next
Would be my final inch –
This gave me that precarious Gait
Some call Experience.

Emily Dickinson (1830-1886)

# Oldness

Everything about me is old,
but the love I have
for a beautiful woman.

Everything is old,
from my hair, like ash from a dead fire,
to my face, withered like autumn grass,
lined like parched earth.

My friends and relatives are old,
some, better than me, some, worse.
Some have retired, some are about to.

My world is old;
my mirror reflects ugliness.

My love, however, is a winter bonfire
on the hill of my childhood years.
Here, I keep myself warm,
here, I entertain my phantom lover.
You are the sweetest, Nameri.

But soon I will douse
even this with water,
and go home to sleep.

**Kynpham Sing Nongkynrih** (1964–)

# Pushing Forty

Just before winter
we see the trees show
their true colours:
the mad yellow of chestnuts
two maples like blood sisters
the orange beech
braver than lipstick

Pushing forty, we vow
that when the time comes
rather than wither
ladylike and white
we will henna our hair
like Colette, we too
will be gold and red
and go out
in a last wild blaze

**Alison Fell** (1944–)

## The Voyage of Life

**From *The Crist*, lines 850-866**

Our life is likest a long sea-voyage:
O'er the water cold in our keels we glide.
O'er Ocean-streams, in our stallions of the deep
We drive afar. 'Tis a dreary waste
Of ceaseless surges we sail across,
In this wavering world, o'er wind-swept tracts
Of open sea. Anxious the struggle.
Ere we bring at last our barks to land.
O'er the rough sea-ridges. Our rescue is near;
The Son of God doth safely guide us,
Helps us in to our harbor of refuge;
Shows from the deck the sheltered waters,
Where smoothly to anchor our ancient chargers,
Hold with hawsers our horses of the deep.
Then fix we our hope on that haven of safety
That the Prince of Glory prepared for us all,
The Ruler on high, when He rose to heaven.

**Cynewulf (c. 9th century)**
**Translated by John Duncan Spaeth (1868-1954)**

## Rondeau

Jenny kissed me when we met,
  Jumping from the chair she sat in;
Time, you thief, who love to get
  Sweets into your list, put that in:
Say I'm weary, say I'm sad,
  Say that health and wealth have missed me,
Say I'm growing old, but add,
  Jenny kissed me.

**Leigh Hunt** (1784–1859)

# Day Trip

Two women, seventies, hold hands
on the edge of Essex,
hair in strong nets,
shrieked laughter echoing gulls
as shingle sucks from under feet
easing in brine.

There must be an unspoken point
when the sea feels like
their future. No longer paddling,
ankles submerge in lace,
in satin ripple.
Dress hems darken.

They do not risk their balance
for the shimmering of ships
at the horizon's sweep
as, thigh deep, they inch on
fingers splayed, wrists bent,
learning to walk again.

**Carole Satyamurti (1939-2019)**

## To every thing there is a season

*Ecclesiastes*, chapter 3, verses 1–8

To every thing there is a season, and a time to every
  purpose under the heaven:
A time to be born, and a time to die; a time to plant,
  and a time to pluck up that which is planted;
A time to kill, and a time to heal; a time to break
  down, and a time to build up;
A time to weep, and a time to laugh; a time to
  mourn, and a time to dance;
A time to cast away stones, and a time to gather
  stones together; a time to embrace, and a
    time to refrain from embracing;
A time to get, and a time to lose; a time to keep, and
  a time to cast away;
A time to rend, and a time to sew; a time to keep
  silence, and a time to speak;
A time to love, and a time to hate; a time of war, and
  a time of peace.

King James Bible

# ‘let us welcome peaceful ev’ning in’

The Winter Evening

William Cowper

## Life!
### Verse 3

Life! we've been long together,
Through pleasant and through cloudy weather;
'Tis hard to part when friends are dear;
Perhaps 'twill cost a sigh, a tear;
Then steal away, give little warning,
  Choose thine own time;
Say not 'Good-night', but in some brighter clime
  Bid me 'Good morning'.

**Anna Laetitia Barbauld** (1743–1825)

# The Happy Life

No silks have I, no furs nor feathers,
But one old gown that knows all weathers;
No veils nor parasols nor lace,
But rough hands and a tanned face.
Yet the soft, crinkled leaves are mine
Where pale, mysterious veins shine,
And laced larches upon the blue,
And grey veils where the moon looks through;
The cries of birds across the lawns
In dark and teeming April dawns;
The sound of wings at the door-sill,
Where grows the wet-eyed tormentil;
The ripe berry's witcheries –
Its perfect round that satisfies;
And the gay scent of the wood I burn,
And the slap of butter in a busy churn.

**Mary Webb (1881-1927)**

# He had his dream

He had his dream, and all through life,
Worked up to it through toil and strife.
Afloat fore'er before his eyes,
It colored for him all his skies:
  The storm-cloud dark
  Above his bark,
The calm and listless vault of blue
Took on its hopeful hue,
It tinctured every passing beam –
  He had his dream.

He labored hard and failed at last,
His sails too weak to bear the blast,
The raging tempests tore away
And sent his beating bark astray.
  But what cared he
  For wind or sea!
He said, 'The tempest will be short,
My bark will come to port.'
He saw through every cloud a gleam –
  He had his dream.

**Paul Laurence Dunbar** (1872-1906)

## Young men dancing, and the old

Young men dancing, and the old
Sporting I with joy behold;
But an old man gay and free
Dancing most I love to see;
Age and youth alike he shares,
For his heart belies his hairs.

Thomas Stanley (1625-1678)

## When You Are Old

When you are old and grey and full of sleep,
And nodding by the fire, take down this book,
And slowly read, and dream of the soft look
Your eyes had once, and of their shadows deep;

How many loved your moments of glad grace,
And loved your beauty with love false or true,
But one man loved the pilgrim soul in you,
And loved the sorrows of your changing face;

And bending down beside the glowing bars,
Murmur, a little sadly, how Love fled
And paced upon the mountains overhead
And hid his face amid a crowd of stars.

**W. B. Yeats (1865-1939)**

## Youth in Age

When younger women stand a breathing space
  Before their mirrors, with an inward smile
  At burnished hair or slender throat or wile
Of dimpled chin, or nest a rose in lace
And note how perfectly it mates the face,
  I, pallid, worn and hollow-templed, pile
  My heart with thoughts of secret triumphs, while
Young hopes are mine, young bliss and youth's light
 pace.

For when my lover's eyes are fixed on me
  There are no years, no hollows, no gray days,
    No harsh realities, no endless prose;
But only flowery lanes of poetry,
  Through which we wander, lost in sweet amaze
    That life could hold such fairness near its close.

**Ethelwyn Wetherald** (1857–1940)

# The Old Woman

As a white candle
  In a holy place,
So is the beauty
  Of an aged face.

As the spent radiance
  Of the winter sun,
So is a woman
  With her travail done.

Her brood gone from her,
  And her thoughts as still
As the waters
  Under a ruined mill.

**Joseph Campbell (1879-1944)**

## Autumn

He told his life story to Mrs. Courtly
Who was a widow. 'Let us get married shortly,'
He said. 'I am no longer passionate,
But we can have some conversation before it is
  too late.'

**Stevie Smith** (1902–1971)

# Life

## From 'The Three Best Things'

Let me but live my life from year to year,
  With forward face and unreluctant soul;
  Not hurrying to, nor turning from the goal;
Not mourning for the things that disappear
In the dim past, nor holding back in fear
  From what the future veils; but with a whole
  And happy heart, that pays its toll
To Youth and Age, and travels on with cheer.

So let the way wind up the hill or down,
  O'er rough or smooth, the journey will be joy:
  Still seeking what I sought when but a boy,
New friendship, high adventure, and a crown,
My heart will keep the courage of the quest,
And hope the road's last turn will be the best.

**Henry Van Dyke (1852-1933)**

# ‘Friendship never knows decay’

**New Friends and Old Friends**
Joseph Parry

# Fare Well

When I lie where shades of darkness
Shall no more assail mine eyes,
Nor the rain make lamentation
  When the wind sighs;
How will fare the world whose wonder
Was the very proof of me?
Memory fades, must the remembered
  Perishing be?

Oh, when this my dust surrenders
Hand, foot, lip, to dust again,
May these loved and loving faces
  Please other men!
May the rusting harvest hedgerow
Still the Traveller's Joy entwine,
And as happy children gather
  Posies once mine.

Look thy last on all things lovely,
Every hour. Let no night
Seal thy sense in deathly slumber
  Till to delight
Thou have paid thy utmost blessing;
Since that all things thou wouldst praise
Beauty took from those who loved them
  In other days.

**Walter de la Mare (1873-1956)**

# Tell the Dear Old Body

Tell the dear old body
  This day I cannot run,
  For the pots are boiling over
  And the mutton isn't done.

Louisa May Alcott (1832-1888)

# Mother and Daughter

XVII

And how could I grow old while she's so young?
  Methinks her heart sets tune for mine to beat,
  We are so near; her new thoughts, incomplete,
Find their shaped wording happen on my tongue;
Like bloom on last year's winterings newly sprung
  My youth upflowers with hers, and must repeat
  Old joyaunces in me nigh obsolete.
Could I grow older while my child's so young?

And there are tales how youthful blood instilled
  Thawing frore Age's veins gave life new course,
And quavering limbs and eyes made indolent
  Grew freshly eager with beginning force:
She so breathes impulse. Were my years twice spent,
Not burdening Age, with her, could make me chilled.

Augusta Webster (1837-1894)

# The Echoing Green
## Verses 1–2

The Sun does arise,
And make happy the skies.
The merry bells ring
To welcome the Spring.
The sky-lark and thrush,
The birds of the bush,
Sing louder around,
To the bells' cheerful sound.
While our sports shall be seen
On the Echoing Green.

Old John, with white hair
Does laugh away care,
Sitting under the oak,
Among the old folk,
They laugh at our play,
And soon they all say.
'Such, such were the joys.
When we all girls & boys,
In our youth-time were seen,
On the Echoing Green.'

**William Blake (1757–1827)**

## The Barn Window

The old barn window, John, –
  Do you remember it, –
How just above it, on the beam,
  The tame doves used to sit,
And how we watched the sunshine stream
  Through motes and gossamer,
When down they fluttered, John,
  With such a breezy whirr?

I think the sunsets, John,
  Are seldom now as red;
They used to linger like a crown
  Upon your auburn head.
From the high hayloft looking down
  To tell me of the nest
The white hen hid there, John, –
  The whole brood's handsomest!

Those times were pleasant, John,
  When we were boy and girl,
Though modern young folk style them 'slow';
  Alack! a giddy whirl
The poor old world is spinning now,
  To stop, who guesses when?
Be thankful with me, John,
  That we were children then!

Have you forgotten, John,
  That Wednesday afternoon
When the great doors were opened wide,
  And all the scents of June
Came in to greet us, side by side,
  In the high-seated swing,
Where flocks of swallows, John,
  Fanned us with startled wing?

Up to the barn eaves, John,
  We swung, two happy things,
At home and careless in the air
  As if we both had wings.
The mountain-side lay far and fair,
  Beyond the blue stream's shore;
I cried, 'Swing higher, John!'
  And fell upon the floor.

Next time I saw you, John,
  You stood beside my bed;
Tears trembled in your clear boy-glance, –
  I thought that I was dead,
But felt my childish pulses dance
  To be beside you still:
I lived to love you, John,
  As to the end I will.

We swing no longer, John;
  We sit at our own door,
And watch the shadows on the hill,
  The sunshine on the shore.
But the window in the barn is still
  A magic-glass to me;
For through its cobwebs, John,
  Our childhood's days I see.

**Lucy Larcom (1824-1893)**

# Optimism

I'm no reformer; for I see more light
Than darkness in the world; mine eyes are quick
To catch the first dim radiance of the dawn,
And slow to note the cloud that threatens storm.
The fragrance and the beauty of the rose
Delight me so, slight thought I give its thorn;
And the sweet music of the lark's clear song
Stays longer with me than the night hawk's cry.
And e'en in this great throe of pain called Life,
I find a rapture linked with each despair,
Well worth the price of Anguish. I detect
More good than evil in humanity.
Love lights more fires than hate extinguishes,
And men grow better as the world grows old.

**Ella Wheeler Wilcox (1850–1919)**

# The Passionate Man's Pilgrimage

*Supposed to be Written by One at the Point of Death*

Lines 1-18

Give me my scallop shell of quiet,
My staff of faith to walk upon,
My scrip of joy, immortal diet,
My bottle of salvation,
My gown of glory, hope's true gage,
And thus I'll take my pilgrimage.

Blood must be my body's balmer,
No other balm will there be given,
Whilst my soul, like a white palmer,
Travelleth to the land of heaven;
Over the silver mountains,
Where spring the nectar fountains.
And there I will kiss
The bowl of bliss,
And drink my eternal fill
On every milken hill.
My soul will be adry before,
But after, it will thirst no more.

**Sir Walter Raleigh** (1552-1618)

## Crossing the Bar

Sunset and evening star,
    And one clear call for me!
And may there be no moaning of the bar,
    When I put out to sea,

  But such a tide as moving seems asleep,
    Too full for sound and foam,
When that which drew from out the boundless deep
    Turns again home.

  Twilight and evening bell,
    And after that the dark!
And may there be no sadness of farewell,
    When I embark;

  For tho' from out our bourne of Time and Place
    The flood may bear me far,
I hope to see my Pilot face to face
    When I have crost the bar.

**Alfred, Lord Tennyson** (1809-1892)

'Crossing the Bar' was written in my father's eighty-first year, on a day in October when we came from Aldworth to Farringford. Before reaching Farringford he had the Moaning of the Bar in his mind, and after dinner he showed me this poem written out.

I said, 'That is the crown of your life's work.' He answered, 'It came in a moment.' He explained the 'Pilot' as 'That Divine and Unseen Who is always guiding us.'

Extract from *A Memoir Vol. II* (1897)
Hallam Tennyson (1852–1928)

'The same yet different, different yet the same'

**Another and Another**
James Henry

# The Seven Ages of Elf-hood

When an elf is as old as a year and a minute
He can wear a cap with a feather in it.

By the time that he is two times two
He has a buckle for either shoe.

At twenty he is as fine as a fiddle,
With a little brown belt to go round his middle.

When he's lived for fifty years or so
His coat may have buttons all in a row.

If past three score and ten he's grown
Two pockets he has for his very own.

At eighty-two or three years old
They bulge and jingle with bits of gold.

But when he's a hundred and a day
He gets a little pipe to play!

**Rachel Field (1894-1942)**

## Youth, and Age

God on our Youth bestowes but little ease;
But on our Age most sweet *Indulgences*.

Robert Herrick (1591-1674)

# So, We'll Go No More a Roving

I

So, we'll go no more a roving
    So late into the night,
Though the heart be still as loving
    And the moon be still as bright.

II

For the sword outwears its sheath,
    And the soul outwears the breast,
And the heart must pause to breathe,
    And love itself have rest.

III

Though the night was made for loving,
    And the day returns too soon,
Yet we'll go no more a roving
    By the light of the moon.

**George Gordon, Lord Byron (1788-1824)**

## New Friends and Old Friends

Make new friends, but keep the old;
Those are silver, these are gold.
New-made friendships, like new wine,
Age will mellow and refine.
Friendships that have stood the test –
Time and change – are surely best;
Brow may wrinkle, hair grow gray,
Friendship never knows decay.
For 'mid old friends, tried and true,
Once more we our youth renew.
But old friends, alas! may die,
New friends must their place supply.
Cherish friendship in your breast –
New is good, but old is best;
Make new friends, but keep the old;
Those are silver, these are gold.

**Joseph Parry (1841-1903)**

# The Optimist

The optimist builds himself safe inside a cell
and paints the inside walls sky-blue
and blocks up the door
and says he's in heaven.

D. H. Lawrence (1885-1930)

# Warning

When I am an old woman I shall wear purple
With a red hat which doesn't go, and doesn't suit me.
And I shall spend my pension on brandy and
  summer gloves
And satin sandals, and say we've no money for butter.
I shall sit down on the pavement when I'm tired
And gobble up samples in shops and press alarm bells
And run my stick along the public railings
And make up for the sobriety of my youth.
I shall go out in my slippers in the rain
And pick the flowers in other people's gardens
And learn to spit.

You can wear terrible shirts and grow more fat
And eat three pounds of sausages at a go
Or only bread and pickle for a week
And hoard pens and pencils and beermats and things
  in boxes.

But now we must have clothes that keep us dry
And pay our rent and not swear in the street
And set a good example for the children.
We must have friends to dinner and read the papers.

But maybe I ought to practise a little now?
So people who know me are not too shocked and
  surprised
When suddenly I am old, and start to wear purple.

**Jenny Joseph** (1932–2018)

# ‘Young hopes are mine’

**Youth in Age**
Ethelwyn Wetherald

## Good-bye

Sounds of the seas grow fainter,
  Sounds of the sands have sped;
The sweep of gales,
The far white sails,
  Are silent, spent and dead.

Sounds of the days of summer
  Murmur and die away,
And distance hides
The long, low tides,
  As night shuts out the day.

E. Pauline Johnson/Tekahionwake (1861-1913)

# The Retirement

## Stanzes Irreguliers, To Mr Izaak Walton
## Stanzas 1–3

Farewell, thou busy world, and may
We never meet again:
Here I can eat, and sleep, and pray,
And do more good in one short day,
Than he who his whole age out wears
Upon thy most conspicuous theatres,
Where naught but vice and vanity do reign.

Good God! how sweet are all things here!
How beautiful the fields appear!
How cleanly do we feed and lie!
Lord! what good hours do we keep!
How quietly we sleep!
What peace! what unanimity!
How innocent from the lewd fashion
Is all our bus'ness, all our conversation!

O how happy here's our leisure!
O how innocent our pleasure!
O ye valleys! O ye mountains!
O ye groves and crystal fountains,
How I love at liberty,
By turn to come and visit ye!

Charles Cotton (1630–1687)

# Why Should Not Old Men Be Mad?

Why should not old men be mad?
Some have known a likely lad
That had a sound fly-fisher's wrist
Turn to a drunken journalist;
A girl that knew all Dante once
Live to bear children to a dunce;
A Helen of social welfare dream,
Climb on a wagonette to scream.
Some think it a matter of course that chance
Should starve good men and bad advance,
That if their neighbours figured plain,
As though upon a lighted screen,
No single story would they find
Of an unbroken happy mind,
A finish worthy of the start.
Young men know nothing of this sort
Observant old men know it well;
And when they know what old books tell
And that no better can be had
Know why an old man should be mad.

**W. B. Yeats** (1865–1939)

## Wisdom

When I have ceased to break my wings
Against the faultiness of things,
And learned that compromises wait
Behind each hardly opened gate,
When I have looked Life in the eyes,
Grown calm and very coldly wise,
Life will have given me the Truth,
And taken in exchange – my youth.

**Sara Teasdale (1884-1933)**

## Prayer to Diana
### Verses 1 and 5

Since thou and the stars, my dear goddess, decree,
That old mid as I am, an old maid I must be,
O! hear the petition I offer to thee,
  For to bear it must be my endeavour;
From the grief of my friendships, all dropping around,
Till not one whom I loved in my youth can be found,
From the legacy-hunters that near us abound,
  Diana, thy servant deliver!

. . . . . .

From spleen at beholding the young more caressed,
From pettish asperity, tartly expressed,
From scandal, detraction, and every such pest,
  From all thy true servant deliver;
Nor let satisfaction depart from her lot,
Let her sing, if at ease, and be patient, if not,
Be pleased when regarded, content when forgot,
  Till fate her slight thread shall dissever.

Mary Tighe (1772-1810)

## Getting Older

The first surprise: I like it.
Whatever happens now, some things
that used to terrify have not:

I didn't die young, for instance. Or lose
my only love. My three children
never had to run away from anyone.

Don't tell me this gratitude is complacent.
We all approach the edge of the same blackness
which for me is silent.

Knowing as much sharpens
my delight in January freesia,
hot coffee, winter sunlight. So we say

as we lie close on some gentle occasion:
every day won from such
darkness is a celebration.

**Elaine Feinstein** (1930-2019)

‘Yet hope again elastic springs’

**Life**
Charlotte Brontë

# Pray do not mock
## From *King Lear*, Act IV, scene vii

*Lear* Pray do not mock me:
I am a very foolish fond old man,
Fourscore and upward, not an hour more nor less;
And, to deal plainly,
I fear I am not in my perfect mind.
Methinks I should know you and know this man;
Yet I am doubtful: for I am mainly ignorant
What place this is, and all the skill I have
Remembers not these garments; nor I know not
Where I did lodge last night. Do not laugh at me;
For, as I am a man, I think this lady
To be my child Cordelia.
*Cordelia* And so I am, I am.

**William Shakespeare (1564-1616)**

## Another and Another

Another and another and another
And still another sunset and sunrise,
The same yet different, different yet the same,
Seen by me now in my declining years
As in my early childhood, youth and manhood;
And by my parents and my parents' parents,
And by the parents of my parents' parents,
And by their parents counted back for ever,
Seen, all their lives long, even as now by me;
And by my children and my children's children
And by the children of my children's children
And by their children counted on for ever
Still to be seen as even now seen by me;
Clear and bright sometimes, sometimes dark
  and clouded
But still the same sunsetting and sunrise;
The same for ever to the never ending
Line of observers, to the same observer
Through all the changes of his life the same:
Sunsetting and sunrising and sunsetting,
And then again sunrising and sunsetting,
Sunrising and sunsetting evermore.

**James Henry (1798-1876)**

# On Himself

Young I was, but now am old,
But I am not yet grown cold;
I can play, and I can twine
'Bout a Virgin like a Vine:
In her lap too I can lye
Melting, and in fancie die:
And return to life, if she
Claps my cheek, or kisseth me;
Thus, and thus it now appears
That our love out-lasts our yeeres.

Robert Herrick (1591-1674)

## Life

Life, believe, is not a dream
  So dark as sages say;
Oft a little morning rain
  Foretells a pleasant day.
Sometimes there are clouds of gloom,
  But these are transient all;
If the shower will make the roses bloom,
  O why lament its fall?
    Rapidly, merrily,
  Life's sunny hours flit by,
    Gratefully, cheerily
  Enjoy them as they fly!

What though Death at times steps in,
  And calls our Best away?
What though sorrow seems to win,
  O'er hope, a heavy sway?
Yet hope again elastic springs,
  Unconquered, though she fell;
Still buoyant are her golden wings,
  Still strong to bear us well.
    Manfully, fearlessly,
  The day of trial bear,
    For gloriously, victoriously,
  Can courage quell despair!

**Charlotte Brontë (1816–1855)**

# The Greatest Love

At sixty she's experiencing
the greatest love of her life.

She walks arm in arm with her lover,
the wind ruffles their grey hairs.

Her lover says:
– You have hair like pearls.

Her children say:
– You silly old fool.

**Anna Świrszczyńska (also known as Anna Swir)**
(1909-1984)

## A Farewell to Arms

His golden locks time hath to silver turn'd;
  O time too swift, O swiftness never ceasing!
His youth 'gainst time and age hath ever spurned,
  But spurned in vain; youth waneth by increasing:
Beauty, strength, youth, are flowers but fading seen;
Duty, faith, love, are roots, and ever green.

His helmet now shall make a hive for bees;
  And, lovers' sonnets turned to holy psalms,
A man-at-arms must now serve on his knees,
  And feed on prayers, which are age's alms:
But though from court to cottage he depart,
His saint is sure of his unspotted heart.

And when he saddest sits in homely cell,
  He'll teach his swains this carol for a song:
'Blest be the hearts that wish my sovereign well,
  Curst be the souls that think her any wrong.'
Goddess, allow this aged man his right,
To be your beadsman now, that was your knight.

George Peele (1556–1596)

## The Grudge of the Old

The old ones want to be young, and they aren't young,
and it rankles, they ache when they see the young,
and they can't help wanting to spite it on them
venomously.

The old ones say to themselves: We are not going to
  be old,
we are not going to make way, we are not going to die,
we are going to stay on and on and on and on and on
and make the young look after us
till they are old. We are stronger than the young.
We have more energy, and our grip on life is harder.
Let us triumph, and let the young be listless
with their puny youth.
We are younger even now than the young, we can
  put their youth in abeyance.

And it is true.
And they do it.
And so it goes on.

**D. H. Lawrence (1885–1930)**

## Sonnets are full of love

Sonnets are full of love, and this my tome
  Has many sonnets: so here now shall be
  One sonnet more, a love sonnet, from me
To her whose heart is my heart's quiet home,
  To my first Love, my Mother, on whose knee
I learnt love-lore that is not troublesome;
  Whose service is my special dignity,
And she my loadstar while I go and come.
And so because you love me, and because
  I love you, Mother, I have woven a wreath
    Of rhymes wherewith to crown your honoured
      name:
    In you not fourscore years can dim the flame
Of love, whose blessed glow transcends the laws
  Of time and change and mortal life and death.

**Christina Rossetti** (1830–1894)

# 'My scrip of joy, immortal diet'

**The Passionate Man's Pilgrimage**
Sir Walter Raleigh

## If No One Ever Marries Me

If no one ever marries me –
  And I don't see why they should,
For nurse says I'm not pretty
  And I'm seldom very good –

If no one ever marries me
  I shan't mind very much;
I shall buy a squirrel in a cage,
  And a little rabbit hutch.

I shall have a cottage near a wood,
  And a pony all my own,
And a little lamb, quite clean and tame,
  That I can take to town.

And when I'm getting really old,
  At twenty eight or nine,
I shall buy a little orphan girl
  And bring her up as mine.

**Laurence Alma-Tadema (c. 1865-1940)**

## L'amitié, est L'amour sans Ailes

### Verse 1

Why should my anxious breast repine,
Because my youth is fled?
Days of delight may still be mine;
Affection is not dead.
In tracing back the years of youth,
One firm record, one lasting truth
Celestial consolation brings;
Bear it, ye breezes, to the seat,
Where first my heart responsive beat, –
'Friendship is Love without his wings!'

George Gordon, Lord Byron (1788–1824)

# Youthing

It's like the process of aging.
Just a process.
Your hair starts to grow wilder,
your skin gets smoother,
your appetites increase.
Suddenly, you sing in the shower and in the rain,
you discover a plant you've never seen before
and you munch it.
What's that tiny star on your left temple?
Maybe a bird scratched it with tender claws
to prod you into flying.
And then, that dialogue with the moon
keeps you awake,
and then, that dream of death
becomes more and more remote
– or is it the other way around?

**Nina Cassian** (1924–2014)

## Fear no more

From *Cymbeline,* Act IV, scene ii

Fear no more the heat o' th' sun,
  Nor the furious winter's rages.
Thou thy worldly task hast done,
  Home art gone, and ta'en thy wages.
Golden lads and girls all must,
As chimney-sweepers, come to dust.

Fear no more the frown o' th' great,
  Thou art past the tyrant's stroke.
Care no more to clothe and eat,
  To thee the reed is as the oak.
The sceptre, learning, physic, must
All follow this and come to dust.

Fear no more the lightning flash,
  Nor th' all-dreaded thunder-stone.
Fear not slander, censure rash.
  Thou hast finished joy and moan.
All lovers young, all lovers must
Consign to thee and come to dust.

No exorciser harm thee,
Nor no witchcraft charm thee,
Ghost unlaid forbear thee.
Nothing ill come near thee.
Quiet consummation have,
And renownèd be thy grave!

**William Shakespeare (1564-1616)**

## Live Your Life

So live your life that the fear of death
can never enter your heart.
Trouble no one about his religion.
Respect others in their views
and demand that they respect yours.
Love your life, perfect your life,
beautify all things in your life.
Seek to make your life long
and of service to your people.
Prepare a noble death song for the day
when you go over the great divide.
Always give a word or a sign of salute when meeting
or passing a friend, or even a stranger, if in a lonely
place.
Show respect to all people but grovel to none.
When you rise in the morning, give thanks for the
light,
for your life, for your strength.

Give thanks for your food and for the joy of living.
If you see no reason to give thanks,
the fault lies in yourself.
Touch not the poisonous firewater that makes wise
ones turn to fools
and robs the spirit of its vision.
When your time comes to die, be not like those
whose hearts are filled with the fear of death,
so that when their time comes they weep and pray
for a little more time to live their lives over again
in a different way.
Sing your death song, and die like a hero going home.

Chief Tecumseh of the Shawnee Nation (1768-1813)

## John Anderson my Jo

John Anderson my jo, John,
  When we were first acquent,
Your locks were like the raven,
  Your bonnie brow was brent;
But now your brow is beld, John,
  Your locks are like the snaw,
But blessings on your frosty pow,
  John Anderson, my jo.

John Anderson my jo, John,
  We clamb the hill thegither,
And mony a canty day, John,
  We've had wi' ane anither;
Now we maun totter down, John,
  And hand in hand we'll go,
And sleep thegither at the foot,
  John Anderson, my jo.

**Robert Burns** (1759-1796)

# Afternoon Tea at the Ritz

When I am old, I shall wear bright red lipstick
and hot pink shoes and outrageous earrings,
and my eyes will sparkle with mischief.
I'll walk a little dog with a fiendish grin that says
*I might be small, but don't mess with me.*
And I'll book tables for two, for me and my pooch,
and order huge pots of tea and chocolate cake;
and waiters will fall over themselves to wait on me.
I shall people-watch, with an indulgent air
in places like *Betty's Tea Room* or *The Ritz*,
and with impunity, stare – because eccentric
old ladies can get away with things.

Gravity will have taken its course, and my face
will be a map of wrinkles, of course;
but frankly, my dears, who cares? I'll have *lived*
and my visage will bear testament to this.
I shall be fearsome and quite magnificent,
for I'll not beat about the bush
but speak the plain un-sugared truth. And yet,
at times, I shall be as soft as cotton wool:
a bosom to cry on; a well of wisdom; an oracle.
Because old folk have seen it all,
don't you know? One must not forget,
they were young once, too.

**Jana Synková (1968–)**

# Retirement

O, let me be alone awhile,
  No human form is nigh.
And may I sing and muse aloud,
  No mortal ear is by.

Away! ye dreams of earthly bliss,
  Ye earthly cares begone:
Depart! ye restless wandering thoughts,
  And let me be alone!

One hour, my spirit, stretch thy wings,
  And quit this joyless sod,
Bask in the sunshine of the sky,
  And be alone with God!

**Anne Brontë (1820-1849)**

# 'our love out-lasts our yeeres'

**On Himself**
Robert Herrick

# Dedicatory Ode

## Part 1

I mean to write with all my strength
   (It lately has been sadly waning)
A ballad of enormous length –
   Some parts of which will need explaining. (1)

Because (unlike the bulk of men
   Who write for fame or public ends)
I turn a lax and fluent pen
   To talking of my private friends. (2)

For no one, in our long decline,
So dusty, spiteful and divided,
Had quite such pleasant friends as mine,
Or loved them half as much as I did.

.   .   .   .   .

(1) But do not think I shall explain
   To any great extent. Believe me,
I partly write to give you pain,
   And if you do not like me, leave me.

(2) And least of all can you complain,
   Reviewers, whose unholy trade is,
To puff with all your might and main
   Biographers of single ladies.

**Hilaire Belloc (1870–1953)**

# The Old Man's Wish

If I live to be old, for I find I go down,
Let this be my fate: in a country town
May I have a warm house, with a stone at the gate,
And a cleanly young girl to rub my bald pate.
  May I govern my passion with an absolute sway,
  And grow wiser and better as my strength wears
    away,
  Without gout or stone, by a gentle decay.

Near a shady grove, and a murmuring brook,
With the ocean at distance, whereupon I may look,
With a spacious plain without hedge or stile,
And an easy pad-nag to ride out a mile.
  May I govern my passion with an absolute sway,
  And grow wiser and better as my strength wears
    away,
  Without gout or stone, by a gentle decay.

With Horace and Petrarch, and two or three more
Of the best wits that lived in the ages before,
With roast mutton, not ven'son or teal,
And clean, though coarse linen, at every meal.
  May I govern my passion with an absolute sway,
  And grow wiser and better as my strength wears
    away,
  Without gout or stone, by a gentle decay.

With a pudding on Sunday, with stout humming
  liquor,
And remnants of Latin to puzzle the Vicar,
With a hidden reserve of Burgundy wine,
To drink the king's health as oft as I dine.
  May I govern my passion with an absolute sway,
  And grow wiser and better as my strength wears
    away,
  Without gout or stone, by a gentle decay.

I hope I shall have no occasion to send
For priests or physicians, till I'm so near my end,
That I have eat all my bread and drank my last glass,
Let them come then and set their seals to my pass.
  May I govern my passion with an absolute sway,
  And grow wiser and better as my strength wears
    away,
  Without gout or stone, by a gentle decay.

With courage undaunted may I face my last day,
And when I am dead may the better sort say,
In the morning when sober, in the evening when
  mellow,
He's gone, and has left not behind him his fellow;
   For he governed his passion with an absolute sway,
   And grew wiser and better as his strength wears
      away,
   Without gout or stone, by a gentle decay.

**Walter Pope** (c. 1627–1714)

‘Touch us gently, gentle Time!’

**A Petition to Time**
Bryan Waller Procter

## Faded
### From 'Retrospection'

We wove a web in childhood,
  A web of sunny air;
We dug a spring in infancy
  Of water pure and fair;

We sowed in youth a mustard seed,
  We cut an almond rod;
We are now grown up to riper age –
  Are they withered in the sod?

Are they blighted, failed and faded,
  Are they mouldered back to clay?
For life is darkly shaded;
  And its joys fleet fast away.

Faded! the web is still of air,
  But how its folds are spread,
And from its tints of crimson clear
  How deep a glow is shed.
The light of an Italian sky.
Where clouds of sunset lingering lie
  Is not more ruby-red.

Charlotte Brontë (1816–1855)

# I Remember, I Remember

I remember, I remember,
The house where I was born,
The little window where the sun
Came peeping in at morn;
He never came a wink too soon,
Nor brought too long a day,
But now, I often wish the night
Had borne my breath away!

I remember, I remember,
The roses, red and white,
The vi'lets, and the lily-cups,
Those flowers made of light!
The lilacs where the robin built,
And where my brother set
The laburnum on his birthday, –
The tree is living yet!

I remember, I remember,
Where I used to swing,
And thought the air must rush as fresh
To swallows on the wing;
My spirit flew in feathers then,
That is so heavy now,
And summer pools could hardly cool
The fever on my brow!

I remember, I remember,
The fir trees dark and high;
I used to think their slender tops
Were close against the sky:
It was a childish ignorance,
But now 'tis little joy
To know I'm farther off from heav'n
Than when I was a boy.

Thomas Hood (1799-1845)

## The Garden-chair: Two Portraits
### Verse 1

A pleasant picture, full of meanings deep,
Old age, calm sitting in the July sun,
On wither'd hands half-leaning – feeble hands,
That after their life-labours, light or hard,
Their girlish broideries, their marriage-ring'd
Domestic duties, their sweet cradle cares,
Have dropped into the quiet-folded ease
Of fourscore years. How peacefully the eyes
Face us! Contented, unregretful eyes,
That carry in them the whole tale of life
With its one moral – 'Thus all was – thus best.'
Eyes now so near unto their closing mild
They seem to pierce direct through all that maze,
As eyes immortal do.

Here – Youth. She stands
Under the roses, with elastic foot
Poised to step forward; eager-eyed, yet grave
Beneath the mystery of the unknown To-come,
Though longing for its coming. Firm prepared
(So say the lifted head and close, sweet mouth)
For any future: though the dreamy hope
Throned on her girlish forehead, whispers fond,
'Surely they err who say that life is hard;
Surely it shall not be with me as these.'

God knows: He only. And so best, dear child,
Thou woman-statured, sixteen-year-old child,
Meet bravely the impenetrable Dark
Under thy roses. Bud and blossom thou
Fearless as they – if thou art planted safe,
Whether for gathering or for withering, safe
In the King's garden.

**Dinah Maria Craik** (1826–1887)

## To Anna

Sister, dear, when you are lonely,
  Longing for your distant home,
And the images of loved ones
  Warmly to your heart shall come,
Then, mid tender thoughts and fancies,
  Let one fond voice say to thee,
'Ever when your heart is heavy,
  Anna, dear, then think of me.'

Think how we two have together
  Journeyed onward day by day,
Joys and sorrows ever sharing,
  While the swift years roll away.
Then may all the sunny hours
  Of our youth rise up to thee,
And when your heart is light and happy,
  Anna, dear, then think of me.

**Louisa May Alcott** (1832–1888)

## Old Age

I have four pairs of glasses:
One for reading, another for distance,
The third for watching breaking news,
And the fourth, I don't remember.
I have learned to live without –
My eyes.

Ashwani Kumar (1965–)

‘He saw through every cloud a gleam’

**He had his dream**
Paul Laurence Dunbar

## What lips my lips have kissed

What lips my lips have kissed, and where, and why,
I have forgotten, and what arms have lain
Under my head till morning; but the rain
Is full of ghosts tonight, that tap and sigh
Upon the glass and listen for reply,
And in my heart there stirs a quiet pain
For unremembered lads that not again
Will turn to me at midnight with a cry.
Thus in the winter stands the lonely tree,
Nor knows what birds have vanished one by one,
Yet knows its boughs more silent than before:
I cannot say what loves have come and gone,
I only know that summer sang in me
A little while, that in me sings no more.

**Edna St Vincent Millay** (1892–1950)

# Terminus

It is time to be old,
To take in sail: –
The god of bounds,
Who sets to seas a shore,
Come to me in his fatal rounds,
And said: 'No more!
No farther shoot
Thy broad ambitious branches, and thy root.
Fancy departs; no more invent;
Contract thy firmament
To compass of a tent.
There's not enough for this and that,
Make thy option which of two;
Economize the failing river,
Not the less revere the Giver,
Leave the many and hold the few.
Timely wise accept the terms,
Soften the fall with wary foot;
A little while
Still plan and smile,
And, fault of novel germs,
Mature the unfallen fruit.

Curse, if thou wilt, thy sires,
Bad husbands of their fires,
Who, when they gave thee breath,
Failed to bequeath
The needful sinew stark as once.
The Baresark marrow to thy bones,
But left a legacy of ebbing veins,
Inconstant heat and nerveless reins, –
Amid the Muses, left thee deaf and dumb,
Amid the gladiators, halt and numb.'

As the bird trims her to the gale,
I trim myself to the storm of time,
I man the rudder, reef the sail,
Obey the voice at eve obeyed at prime:
'Lowly faithful, banish fear,
Right onward drive unharmed;
The port, well worth the cruise, is near,
And every wave is charmed.'

**Ralph Waldo Emerson (1803-1882)**

## The Winter Evening

### From *The Task*, Book IV, lines 36–41

Now stir the fire, and close the shutters fast,
Let fall the curtains, wheel the sofa round,
And, while the bubbling and loud-hissing urn
Throws up a steamy column, and the cups,
That cheer but not inebriate, wait on each,
So let us welcome peaceful ev'ning in.

William Cowper (1731-1800)

## Though you are yoong

Though you are yoong and I am olde,
Though your vaines hot and my bloud colde,
Though youth is moist and age is drie,
Yet embers live when flames doe die.

The tender graft is easely broke,
But who shall shake the sturdie Oke?
You are more fresh and faire than I,
Yet stubs do live, when flowers doe die.

Thou, that thy youth doest vainly boast,
Know buds are soonest nipt with frost;
Thinke that thy fortune still doth crie:
Thou foole, tomorrow thou must die.

**Thomas Campion** (1567-1620)

## Keep Right on to the End of the Road

Every road through life is a long, long road
Filled with joys and sorrows too
As you journey on how your heart may yearn
For the things most dear to you
With wealth and love 'tis so
But onward we must go

*Keep right on to the end of the road*
*Keep right on to the end*
*Though the way be long, let your heart be strong*
*Keep right on round the bend*
*Though you're tired and weary still journey on*
*Till you come to your happy abode*
*Where all your love and your dreaming of*
*Will be there at the end of the road*

With a big stout heart to a long steep hill
We may get there with a smile
With a good kind thought and an end in view
We can cut short many a mile
So let courage every day
Be your guiding star always

*Keep right on . . . . . .*

**Harry Lauder** (1870–1950)

## The Prayer of the Year

Leave me Hope when I am old;
  Strip my joys from me,
Let November to the cold
  Bare each leafy tree;
Chill my lover, dull my friend,
  Only, while I grope
To the dark, the silent end,
  Leave me Hope!

Blight my bloom when I am old,
  Bid my sunlight cease;
If it need be, from my hold
  Take the hand of Peace.
Leave no springtime memory,
  But upon the slope
Of the days that are to be,
  Leave me Hope!

**Ethelwyn Wetherald (1857-1940)**

## Love and Age

I played with you 'mid cowslips blowing,
When I was six and you were four;
When garlands weaving, flower-balls throwing,
Were pleasures soon to please no more.
Through groves and meads, o'er grass and heather,
With little playmates, to and fro,
We wandered hand in hand together;
But that was sixty years ago.

You grew a lovely roseate maiden,
And still our early love was strong;
Still with no care our days were laden,
They glided joyously along;
And I did love you, very dearly,
How dearly words want power to show;
I thought your heart was touched as nearly;
But that was fifty years ago.

Then other lovers came around you,
Your beauty grew from year to year,
And many a splendid circle found you
The centre of its glistening sphere.
I saw you then, first vows forsaking,
On rank and wealth your hand bestow;
Oh, then I thought my heart was breaking, –
But that was forty years ago.

And I lived on, to wed another:
No cause she gave me to repine;
And when I heard you were a mother,
I did not wish the children mine.
My own young flock, in fair progression,
Made up a pleasant Christmas row:
My joy in them was past expression; –
But that was thirty years ago.

You grew a matron plump and comely,
You dwelt in fashion's brightest blaze;
My earthly lot was far more homely;
But I too had my festal days.
No merrier eyes have ever glistened
Around the hearth-stone's wintry glow,
Than when my youngest child was christened: –
But that was twenty years ago.

Time passed. My eldest girl was married,
And now I am a grandsire grey;
One pet of four years old I've carried
Among the wild-flowered meads to play.
In our old fields of childish pleasure,
Where now as then, the cowslips blow,
She fills her basket's ample measure, –
And that is not ten years ago.

But though love's first impassioned blindness
Has passed away in colder light,
I still have thought of you with kindness,
And shall do, till our last good-night.
The ever-rolling silent hours
Will bring a time we shall not know,
When our young days of gathering flowers
Will be a hundred years ago.

Thomas Love Peacock (1785–1866)

# ‘To every thing there is a season’

**To every thing there is a season**
King James Bible

## Do not go gentle into that good night

Do not go gentle into that good night,
Old age should burn and rave at close of day;
Rage, rage against the dying of the light.

Though wise men at their end know dark is right,
Because their words had forked no lightning they
Do not go gentle into that good night.

Good men, the last wave by, crying how bright
Their frail deeds might have danced in a green bay,
Rage, rage against the dying of the light.

Wild men who caught and sang the sun in flight,
And learn, too late, they grieved it on its way,
Do not go gentle into that good night.

Grave men, near death, who see with blinding sight
Blind eyes could blaze like meteors and be gay,
Rage, rage against the dying of the light.

And you, my father, there on the sad height,
Curse, bless, me now with your fierce tears, I pray.
Do not go gentle into that good night.
Rage, rage against the dying of the light.

**Dylan Thomas (1914–1953)**

## Two Old Women

The two of us sit in the doorway,
chatting about our children and grandchildren.
We sink happily
into our oldwomanhood.

Like two spoons
sinking
into a bowl of hot porridge.

Anna Świrszczyńska (also known as Anna Swir)
(1909-1984)

# An Antiquated Grace

An antiquated Grace
Becomes that cherished Face
As well as prime
Enjoining us to part
We and our pouting Heart
Good friends with time

Emily Dickinson (1830-1886)

## Fairer than younger beauties, more beloved

Fairer than younger beauties, more beloved
  Than many a wife, –
By stress of Time's vicissitudes unmoved
  From settled calm of life, –

Endearing rectitude to those who watch
  The verdict of your face,
Raising & making gracious those who catch
  A semblance of your grace: –

With kindly lips of welcome, & with pleased
  Propitious eyes benign,
Accept a kiss of homage from your least
  Last Valentine.

**Christina Rossetti** (1830-1894)

## Seven Ages
### From *As You Like It*, Act II, scene vii

All the world's a stage,
And all the men and women merely players.
They have their exits and their entrances,
And one man in his time plays many parts,
His acts being seven ages. At first the infant,
Mewling and puking in the nurse's arms.
Then the whining school-boy with his satchel
And shining morning face, creeping like a snail
Unwillingly to school. And then the lover,
Sighing like a furnace, with a woeful ballad
Made to his mistress' eyebrow. Then a soldier,
Full of strange oaths, and bearded like the pard,
Jealous in honour sudden, and quick in quarrel,
Seeking the bubble reputation
Even in the canon's mouth. And then the justice,

In fair round belly with good capon lined,
With eyes severe and beard of formal cut,
Full of wise saws and modern instances;
And so he plays his part. The sixth age shifts
Into the lean and slippered pantaloon,
With spectacles on nose and pouch on side,
His youthful hose, well saved, a world too wide
For his shrunk shank; and his big, manly voice,
Turning again toward childish treble, pipes
And whistles in his sound. Last scene of all,
That ends this strange, eventful history,
Is second childishness, and mere oblivion,
Sans teeth, sans eyes, sans taste, sans everything.

**William Shakespeare (1564–1616)**

## A Song of a Young Lady, to her Ancient Lover

Ancient person, for whom I
All the flattering youth defy,
Long be it ere thou grow old,
Aching, shaking, crazy, cold;
But still continue as thou art,
        Ancient Person of my heart.

On thy withered lips and dry,
Which like barren furrows lie,
Brooding kisses I will pour
Shall thy youthful heat restore
Such kind showers in autumn fall,
And a second spring recall:
Nor from thee will ever part,
        Ancient Person of my heart.

Thy nobler part, which but to name
In our sex would be counted shame,
By age's frozen grasp possessed,
From [his] ice shall be released,
And, soothed by my reviving hand,
In former warmth and vigour stand.
All a lover's wish can reach
For thy joy my love shall teach,
And for they pleasure shall improve
All that art can add to love.
Yet still I love thee without art,
        Ancient Person of my heart.

**John Wilmot, Lord Rochester (1647-1680)**

# The Last Laugh

I made hay while the sun shone.
  My work sold.
Now, if the harvest is over
  And the world cold,
Give me the bonus of laughter
  As I lose hold.

**John Betjeman** (1906-1984)

## On Aging

When you see me sitting quietly,
Like a sack left on the shelf,
Don't think I need your chattering.
I'm listening to myself.
Hold! Stop! Don't pity me!
Hold! Stop your sympathy!
Understanding if you got it,
Otherwise I'll do without it!

When my bones are stiff and aching,
And my feet won't climb the stair,
I will only ask one favor:
Don't bring me no rocking chair.

When you see me walking, stumbling,
Don't study and get it wrong.
'Cause tired don't mean lazy
And every goodbye ain't gone.
I'm the same person I was back then,
A little less hair, a little less chin,
A lot less lungs and much less wind.
But ain't I lucky I can still breathe in.

**Maya Angelou (1928–2014)**

## Felix Antonius (After Martial)

To-day my friend is seventy-five;
  He tells his tale with no regret;
  His brave old eyes are steadfast yet,
His heart the lightest heart alive.

He sees behind him green and wide
  The pathway of his pilgrim years;
  He sees the shore, and dreadless hears
The whisper of the creeping tide.

For out of all his days, not one
  Has passed and left its unlaid ghost
  To seek a light for ever lost,
Or wail a deed for ever done.

So for reward for life-long truth
  He lives again, as good men can
  Redoubling his allotted span
With memories of a stainless youth.

**Sir Henry Newbolt** (1862–1938)

## A Child to His Sick Grandfather
### Verses 1–2

Grand-dad, they say you're old and frail,
Your stocked legs begin to fail:
Your knobbed stick (that was my horse)
Can scarce support your bended corse;
While back to wall you lean so sad,
  I'm vexed to see you, dad.

You used to smile and stroke my head,
And tell me how good children did;
But now, I wot not how it be,
You take me seldom on your knee;
Yet ne'ertheless I am right glad
  To sit beside you, dad.

Joanna Baillie (1762–1851)

## Mother to Son

Well, son, I'll tell you:
Life for me ain't been no crystal stair.
It's had tacks in it,
And splinters,
And boards torn up,
And places with no carpet on the floor –
Bare.
But all the time
I'se been a-climbin' on,
And reachin' landin's,
And turnin' corners,
And sometimes goin' in the dark
Where there ain't been no light.
So boy, don't you turn back.
Don't you set down on the steps
'Cause you finds it's kinder hard.
Don't you fall now –
For I'se still goin', honey,
I'se still climbin',
And life for me ain't been no crystal stair.

**Langston Hughes (1901-1967)**

## Thanks in Old Age

Thanks in old age – thanks ere I go,
For health, the midday sun, the impalpable air – for life, mere life,
For precious ever-lingering memories, (of you my mother dear – you, father – you, brothers, sisters, friends,)
For all my days – not those of peace alone – the days of war the same,
For gentle words, caresses, gifts from foreign lands,
For shelter, wine and meat – for sweet appreciation,
(You distant, dim unknown – or young or old – countless, unspecified, readers belov'd,
We never met, and ne'er shall meet – and yet our souls embrace, long, close and long;)
For beings, groups, love, deeds, words, books – for colors, forms,
For all the brave strong men – devoted, hardy men – who've forward sprung in freedom's help, all years, all lands,
For braver, stronger, more devoted men – (a special laurel ere I go, to life's war's chosen ones,
The cannoneers of song and thought – the great artillerists – the foremost leaders, captains of the soul:)
As soldier from an ended war return'd – As traveler out of myriads, to the long procession retrospective,
Thanks – joyful thanks! – a soldier's, traveler's thanks.

**Walt Whitman (1819-1892)**

'the heart must pause to breathe'

**So, We'll Go No More a Roving**
George Gordon, Lord Byron

## Life is Too Short

Life is too short for any vain regretting;
Let dead delight bury its dead, I say,
And let us go upon our way forgetting
The joys and sorrows of each yesterday
Between the swift sun's rising and its setting
We have no time for useless tears or fretting:
        Life is too short.

Life is too short for any bitter feeling;
Time is the best avenger if we wait;
The years speed by, and on their wings bear healing;
We have no room for anything like hate.
This solemn truth the low mounds seem revealing
That thick and fast about our feet are stealing:
        Life is too short.

Life is too short for aught but high endeavour –
Too short for spite, but long enough for love.
And love lives on forever and forever;
It links the worlds that circle on above:
'Tis God's first law, the universe's lever.
In His vast realm the radiant souls sigh never
        'Life is too short.'

Ella Wheeler Wilcox (1850-1919)

# Clarinda's Indifference at Parting With Her Beauty

Now, age came on, and all the dismal train
That fright the vicious and afflict the vain.
Departing beauty now Clarinda spies,
Pale in her cheeks and dying in her eyes;
That youthful air that wanders o'er the face,
That undescribed, that unresisted grace,
Those morning beams that strongly warm and shine,
Which men that feel and see can ne'er define,
Now, on the wings of restless time, were fled,
And evening shades began to rise and spread;
When, thus resolved, and ready soon to part,
Slighting the short reprieves of proffered art,
She spake –
'And what, vain beauty, didst thou e'er achieve,
When at thy height, that I thy fall should grieve?
When didst thou e'er successfully pursue?
When didst thou e'er th' appointed foe subdue?
'Tis vain of numbers, or of strength to boast,
In an undisciplined, unguided host,

And love, that did thy mighty hopes deride,
Would pay no sacrifice, but to thy pride.
When didst thou e'er a pleasing rule obtain?
A glorious empire's but a glorious pain.
Thou art, indeed, but vanity's chief source;
But foil to wit, to want of wit a curse:
For often by thy gaudy sign's descried
A fool, which unobserved, had been untried;
And when thou dost such empty things adorn,
'Tis but to make them more the public scorn.
I know thee well, but weak thy reign would be
Did none adore or praise thee more than me.
I see, indeed, thy certain ruin near,
But can't afford one parting sigh or tear,
Nor rail at time, nor quarrel with my glass,
But unconcerned, can let thy glories pass.'

**Anne Finch, Countess of Winchilsea (1661-1720)**

# Faithful Wilson

'I say she's handsome, by all laws
Of beauty, if wife ever was!'
Wilson insists thus, though each day
The years fret Fanny towards decay.
'She *was* once beauteous as a jewel,'
Hint friends; 'but Time, of course, is cruel.'
Still Wilson does not quite feel how,
Once fair, she can be different now.

Thomas Hardy (1840–1928)

## My Heart Leaps Up

My heart leaps up when I behold
  A rainbow in the sky:
So was it when my life began;
So is it now I am a man;
So be it when I shall grow old,
  Or let me die!
The Child is father of the Man;
And I could wish my days to be
Bound each to each by natural piety.

**William Wordsworth** (1770–1850)

# The Old Man's Comforts and How He Gained Them

You are old, Father William, the young man cried,
  The few locks which are left you are grey;
You are hale, Father William, a hearty old man,
  Now tell me the reason I pray.

In the days of my youth, Father William replied,
  I remember'd that youth would fly fast,
And abused not my health and my vigour at first
  That I never might need them at last.

You are old, Father William, the young man cried,
  And pleasures with youth pass away,
And yet you lament not the days that are gone,
  Now tell me the reason I pray.

In the days of my youth, Father William replied,
  I remember'd that youth could not last;
I thought of the future whatever I did,
  That I never might grieve for the past.

You are old, Father William, the young man cried,
  And life must be hastening away;
You are chearful, and love to converse upon death!
  Now tell me the reason I pray.

I am chearful, young man, Father William replied,
  Let the cause thy attention engage;
In the days of my youth I remember'd my God!
  And He hath not forgotten my age.

**Robert Southey** (1774-1843)

## You are old, Father William

'You are old, Father William,' the young man said,
'And your hair has become very white;
And yet you incessantly stand on your head –
Do you think, at your age, it is right?'

'In my youth,' Father William replied to his son,
'I feared it would injure the brain;
But now that I'm perfectly sure I have none,
Why, I do it again and again.'

'You are old,' said the youth, 'as I mentioned before,
And have grown most uncommonly fat;
Yet you turned a back-somersault in at the door –
Pray, what is the reason of that?'

'In my youth,' said the sage, as he shook his grey locks,
'I kept all my limbs very supple
By the use of this ointment – one shilling the box –
Allow me to sell you a couple.'

'You are old,' said the youth, 'and your jaws are too weak
For anything tougher than suet;
Yet you finished the goose, with the bones and the beak –
Pray, how did you manage to do it?'

'In my youth,' said his father, 'I took to the law,
  And argued each case with my wife;
And the muscular strength, which it gave to my jaw,
  Has lasted the rest of my life.'

'You are old,' said the youth; one would hardly suppose
  That your eye was as steady as ever;
Yet you balanced an eel on the end of your nose –
  What made you so awfully clever?'

'I have answered three questions, and that is enough,'
  Said his father; 'don't give yourself airs!
Do you think I can listen all day to such stuff?
  Be off, or I'll kick you down stairs!'

Lewis Carroll (1832-1898)

# Old Age

The seas are quiet when the winds give o'er;
So calm are we when passions are no more.
For then we know how vain it was to boast
Of fleeting things, so certain to be lost.

Clouds of affection from our younger eyes
Conceal that emptiness which age descries.
The soul's dark cottage, batter'd and decay'd,
Lets in new light through chinks that time hath
  made:

Stronger by weakness, wiser men become
As they draw near to their eternal home.
Leaving the old, both worlds at once they view
That stand upon the threshold of the new.

**Edmund Waller** (1606-1687)

# 'lament not the days that are gone'

The Old Man's Comforts and How He Gained Them

Robert Southey

# The Fittest

A young man of twenty-one
Going into hospital
For his first operation
Re-decorated his flat,
Re-hung the door, and arranged
A great deal more cupboard space.

A man of seventy-one
Bought an old manor house cheap
Because of dry rot so wide-
Spread and firmly established
That it would take a lifetime
To eradicate they said.

A man of eighty-two
Was more gallant to pretty
Girls than he had ever been.
He drove right across Europe
And to crown it all adopted
Five orphans, almost babies.

Patricia Beer (1919-1999)

# Old Age

Thou hast been wrong'd, I think old age;
  Thy sovereign reign comes not in wrath,
Thou call'st us home from pilgrimage,
  Spreadest the seat and clear'st the hearth.

The hopes and fears that shook our youth,
  By thee are turn'd to a certainty;
I see my boy become a man,
  I hold my girl's girl on my knee.

Whate'er of good has been, dost thou
  In the departed past make sure;
Whate'er has changed from weal to woe,
  Thy comrade Death stands nigh to cure.

And once or twice in age there shines
  Brief gladness, as when winter weaves
In frosty days o'er naked trees,
  A sudden splendour of white leaves.

The past revives, and thoughts return,
  Which kindled once the youthful breast;
They light us, though no more they burn,
  They turn to grey and are at rest.

Caroline Clive (1801-1873)

## To M.E.W.

Words, for alas my trade is words, a barren burst
 of rhyme,
Rubbed by a hundred rhymesters, battered a
 thousand times,
Take them, you, that smile on strings, those nobler
 sounds than mine,
The words that never lie, or brag, or flatter, or
 malign.

I give a hand to my lady, another to my friend,
To whom you too have given a hand; and so before
 the end
We four may pray, for all the years, whatever suns
 be set,
The sale two prayers worth praying – to live and
 not forget.

The pale leaf falls in pallor, but the green leaf turns
to gold;
We that have found it good to be young shall find
it good to be old;
Life that bringeth the marriage bell, the cradle and
the grave,
Life that is mean to the mean of heart, and only
brave to the brave.

In the calm of the last white winter, when all the past
is ours,
Old tears are frozen as jewels, old storms frosted
as flowers.
Dear Lady, may we meet again, stand up again,
we four,
Beneath the burden of the years, and praise the
earth once more.

**G. K. Chesterton (1874-1936)**

# ‘I see more light than darkness in the world’

**Optimism**
Ella Wheeler Wilcox

## Sonnet 73

That time of year thou mayst in me behold
When yellow leaves, or none, or few, do hang
Upon those boughs which shake against the cold,
Bare ruin'd choirs, where late the sweet birds sang;
In me thou seest the twilight of such day
As after sunset fadeth in the west,
Which by and by black night doth take away,
Death's second self, that seals up all in rest;
In me thou seest the glowing of such fire
That on the ashes of his youth doth lie,
As the deathbed whereon it must expire,
Consumed with that which it was nourished by;
  This thou perceiv'st, which makes thy love more strong,
  To love that well, which thou must leave ere long.

**William Shakespeare (1564-1616)**

## A Song of Success

YOUTH.

I am dancing along. Just to live is a joy,
I'm so happy and free.
I know not nor care what will tame or destroy,
Life now satisfies me.
Oh, there's naught like dear youth
To reveal the glad truth
That 'tis pure, healthful joy just to know and to be!

MIDDLE AGE.

I am marching along, full of work and of plan
To alleviate wrong.
With a heart full of love both to God and to man,
And an arm free and strong.
Oh, there's naught like mid-life
To make sure without strife
The beauty of progress through action and song.

## OLD AGE.

I am living along, sitting down by the way.
My work is all done.
I have fought the good fight, known the full of each day,
And true victory won.
Oh, there's naught like old age
To declare with the sage.
Life ending on earth is but heaven begun.

**Elizabeth Porter Gould** (1848-1906)

## Age to Youth

Sunrise is in your eyes, and in your heart
The hope and bright desire of morn and May.
My eyes are full of shadow, and my part
Of life is yesterday.

Yet lend my hand your hand, and let us sit
And see your life unfolding like a scroll,
Rich with illuminated blazon, fit
For your arm-bearing soul.

My soul bears arms too, but the scroll's rolled tight,
Yet the one strip of faded brightness shown
Proclaims that when 'twas splendid in the light
Its blazon matched your own.

E. Nesbit (1858-1924)

## To Enjoy

### From *The Tragedy of Cleopatra*

Not he that knows how to acquire,
  But to enjoy, is blest.
Nor does our happiness consist
  In motion, but in rest.

The gods pass man in bliss, because
  They toil not for more height;
But can enjoy, and in their own
  Eternal rest delight.

Then, princes, do not toil nor care
  Enjoy what you possess.
Which whilst you do, you equalize
  The gods in happiness.

Thomas May (1594/5-1650)

## Time

***Inscription on the pendulum of the tower clock***
***St Lawrence's Church, Bidborough, Kent***

*When as a child I laughed and wept, time crept.*
When as a youth I dreamed and talked, time walked.
When I became a full grown man, time ran.
And later as I older grew, time flew.
Soon I shall find when travelling on, time gone.
*Will Christ have saved my soul by then? Amen.*

Anon.

## I Shall Live to be Old

I shall live to be old, who feared I should die young,
  I shall live to be old.
I shall cling to life as the leaves to the creaking oak
  In the rustle of falling snow and the cold.

The other trees let loose their leaves on the air
  In their russet and red,
I have lived long enough to wonder which is the best,
  And to envy sometimes the way of the early dead.

Sara Teasdale (1884-1933)

## Late Fragment

And did you get what
you wanted from this life, even so?
I did.
And what did you want?
To call myself beloved, to feel myself
beloved on the earth.

Raymond Carver (1938-1988)

## Halcyon Days

Not from successful love alone,
Nor wealth, nor honor'd middle age, nor victories of
  politics or war;
But as life wanes, and all the turbulent passions calm,
As gorgeous, vapory, silent hues cover the evening
  sky,
As softness, fulness, rest, suffuse the frame, like
  freshier, balmier air,
As the days take on a mellower light, and the apple
  at last hangs really finish'd and indolent-ripe on the
  tree,
Then for the teeming quietest, happiest days of all!
The brooding and blissful halcyon days!

Walt Whitman (1819–1892)

## Looking back

Looking back along life's trodden way
  Gleams and greenness linger on the track;
Distance melts and mellows all today,
  Looking back.

Rose and purple and a silvery grey,
  Is that cloud the cloud we called so black?
Evening harmonizes all today,
  Looking back.

Foolish feet so prone to halt or stray,
  Foolish heart so restive on the rack!
Yesterday we sighed, but not today
  Looking back.

**Christina Rossetti** (1830–1894)

# ‘My heart will keep the courage of the quest’

**Life**
Henry Van Dyke

# Index of poets

# Index of first lines

## Sources

Maya Angelou, 'On Aging' from AND STILL I RISE: A BOOK OF POEMS, copyright © 1978 by Caged Bird Legacy, LLC. Used by permission of Random House, an imprint and division of Penguin Random House LLC. All rights reserved. 'On Aging' from *Maya Angelou: The Complete Poetry* (Virago Press, 2015), reproduced with permission of the Licensor through PLSclear.

Patricia Beer, 'The Fittest' from *Collected Poems* (Carcanet, 1988). Reproduced by permission of Carcanet Press Limited.

John Betjeman, 'The Last Laugh' from *Collected Poems* (John Murray, 1979). Copyright © John Betjeman, 1979.

Raymond Carver, 'Late Fragment' from *All of Us: Collected Poems* (Harvill, 1997), Penguin Random House.

Nina Cassian, 'Youthing' from *Take My Word For It* (Anvil Press, 1998). Reproduced by permission of Carcanet Press Limited. Copyright © 1998 by Nina Cassian. Used by permission of W. W. Norton & Company, Inc.

Elaine Feinstein, 'Getting Older' from *Selected Poems* (Carcanet, 1994). Reproduced by permission of Carcanet Press Limited.

Alison Fell, 'Pushing Forty' from *Kisses for Mayakovsky* (Virago, 1984). Reproduced with permission of the licensor through PLS Clear.

Langston Hughes, 'Mother to Son' from *Selected Poems* (Serpent's Tail, 2020). Copyright © 1994 by The Estate of Langston Hughes. Reprinted by permission of Harold Ober Associates and International Literary Properties LLC.

Jenny Joseph, 'Warning' from *Selected Poems* (Bloodaxe Books, 1992). Copyright © Jenny Joseph, SELECTED POEMS, Bloodaxe 1992. Reproduced with permission of Johnson & Alcock Ltd.

Jackie Kay, 'Promise' from *Darling: New and Selected Poems* (Bloodaxe Books, 2008). Reproduced with permission of Bloodaxe Books. www.bloodaxebooks.com @bloodaxebooks (twitter/facebook) #bloodaxebooks

Ashwani Kumar, 'Old Age' from *Converse: Contemporary English Poetry by Indians* (Pippa Rann Books & Media, 2022). Republished with permission of Ashwani Kumar.

Kynpham Sing Nongkynrih, 'Oldness' from *Converse: Contemporary English Poetry by Indians* (Pippa Rann Books & Media, 2022). Republished with permission of Kynpham Sing Nongkynrih.

Carole Satyamurti, 'Day Trip' from *Stitching in the Dark: New and Selected Poems* (Bloodaxe Books, 2005). Reproduced with permission of Bloodaxe Books. www.bloodaxebooks.com @bloodaxebooks (twitter/facebook) #bloodaxebooks

Stevie Smith, 'Autumn' from *Collected Poems of Stevie Smith* (Faber and Faber Ltd., 2018). Copyright 1942 by Stevie Smith. Reprinted with the permission of The Permissions Company, LLC, on behalf of New Directions Publishing Corp., ndbooks.com.

Anna Swir, 'Her Greatest Love' and 'Two Old Women' from *Fat Like the Sun* (The Women's Press Ltd, 1986) trans. Margaret Marshment and Grazyna Baran.

Jana Synková, 'Afternoon Tea at the Ritz'. Reproduced with kind permission of Jana Synková.

Batsford is committed to respecting the intellectual property rights of others. We have taken all reasonable efforts to ensure that the reproduction of all contents on these pages is done with the full consent of the copyright owners. If you are aware of unintentional omissions, please contact the company directly so that any necessary correction may be made for future editions.

*If you enjoyed this collection,*
*how about trying another in the series?*

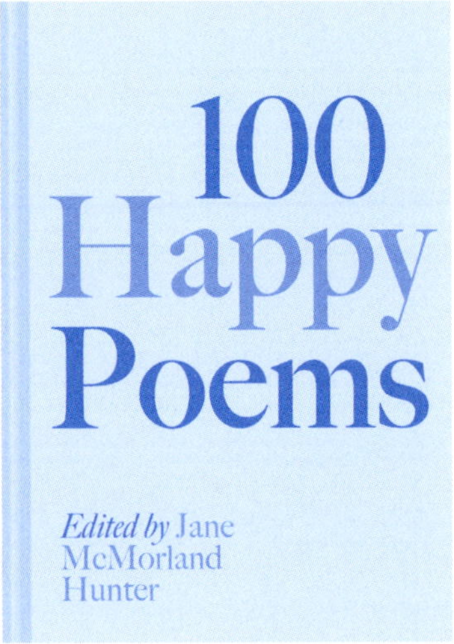


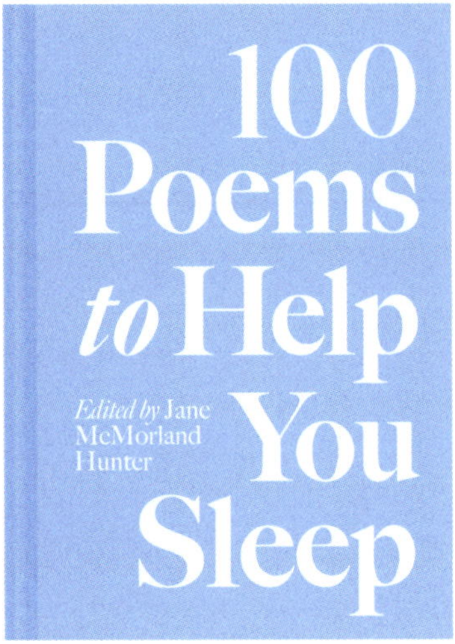

100
Poems
to Help
You
Heal
Edited by
Liz Ison

100
Poems
to Help
You
Relax
Edited by
Liz Ison

Edited by
Liz Ison
100
Poems
to Grow
Your
Confidence

# Acknowledgements

As always I want to thank Hatchards, at Piccadilly, St Pancras and Cheltenham, for looking after my books so well, and everyone at Hatchards Piccadilly in particular, for being so tolerant of the author/editor in their midst. Also, thanks to Alessia, Beth, Chris, Francis, Julia, Julie and Miranda for suggestions. Finally, thanks to my editors Nicola Newman and Magdalen Simões-Brown, and everyone at Batsford who helps with these anthologies.

# About the Editor

Jane McMorland Hunter has compiled anthologies for Batsford and the National Trust including collections on gardening, nature, food, travel, books, London, England and the First World War. She also writes children's, nature, gardening, cookery and craft books and works at Hatchards Bookshop in Piccadilly. At various times she has also worked as a gardener, potter and quilter. She lives in London in a house which is overflowing with books, with a small garden, which is overflowing with plants.

First published in the United Kingdom
in 2026 by
Batsford
43 Great Ormond Street
London
WC1N 3HZ

An imprint of B. T. Batsford Holdings Limited



ISBN 978 1 83733 061 4

A CIP catalogue record for this book is available from the British Library.

10 9 8 7 6 5 4 3 2 1

Printed by Toppan Leefung Printing International Ltd, China
Reproduction by Rival Colour Ltd, UK

This book can be ordered direct from the publisher at www.batsfordbooks.com, or try your local bookshop

Distributed throughout the UK and Europe by Abrams & Chronicle Books, 1st Floor, 22–24 Ely Place, London EC1N 6TE and 57 rue Gaston Tessier, 75166 Paris, France

www.abramsandchronicle.co.uk
info@abramsandchronicle.co.uk

FSC www.fsc.org MIX Paper | Supporting responsible forestry FSC® C104723